CW01373685

THE LIFE
OF PLANTS

Words in *italics* in the main
text (*or in* Roman *type in
the captions*) are explained
in the Index and glossary at
the end of the book.

A Cherrytree Book

Adapted by A S Publishing
from *LA VIDA DE LAS PLANTAS*
by Maria Àngels Julivert
Licenciada en Biología
illustrated by Estudio Marcel Socías
© Parramón Ediciones, S.A. - 1992

This edition first published 1993
by Cherrytree Press Ltd
a subsidiary of
The Chivers Company Ltd
Windsor Bridge Road
Bath, Avon BA2 3AX

© Cherrytree Press Ltd 1993

British Library Cataloguing in Publication Data

Life of Plants. – (Invisible World Series)
 I. Halton, France II. Series
 581

 ISBN 0-7451-5205-8

Typeset by Dorchester Typesetting, Dorset
Printed in Spain

All rights reserved. No part of this publication may be
reproduced, stored in a retrieval system, or transmitted, in
any form or by any means without the prior permission in
writing of the publisher, nor be otherwise circulated in any
form of binding or cover other than that in which it is
published and without a similar condition including this
condition being imposed on the subsequent purchaser.

INVISIBLE WORLD
THE LIFE
OF PLANTS

Edited by
Frances Halton

CHERRYTREE BOOKS

THE LIFE OF PLANTS

Growth

There are more different kinds of plants than you could ever imagine. They vary from tiny organisms with only one cell to giant trees. In this book we are going to look at the kinds of plants that have *roots*, *stems* and *leaves*. Many of them also have *flowers*. They are known as the *higher plants*.

The root anchors the plant to the ground, and takes in water and nutrients, while the leaves trap the sun's energy for the plant to use. The stem supports the plant and acts as a channel for its food.

Unlike animals, which grow until they are mature and then stop, plants continue growing all through their life. New cells are always being formed at the tip, and as these cells grow, the roots and stems get longer.

The roots and stems of plants usually grow thicker as well as longer. New roots grow, often forming a dense mass, and side shoots branch out from the main stem. Some plants grow quickly but others very slowly. Some live for only a few weeks or months, but others for years and years. The largest and longest lived of all plants are trees; some grow to over 80 metres tall, and the oldest we know of has been growing for almost 5000 years.

The higher plants have three main parts: a root, a stem and leaves. From the main root a network of secondary roots fans out, and a number of branches may grow from the stem. ▶

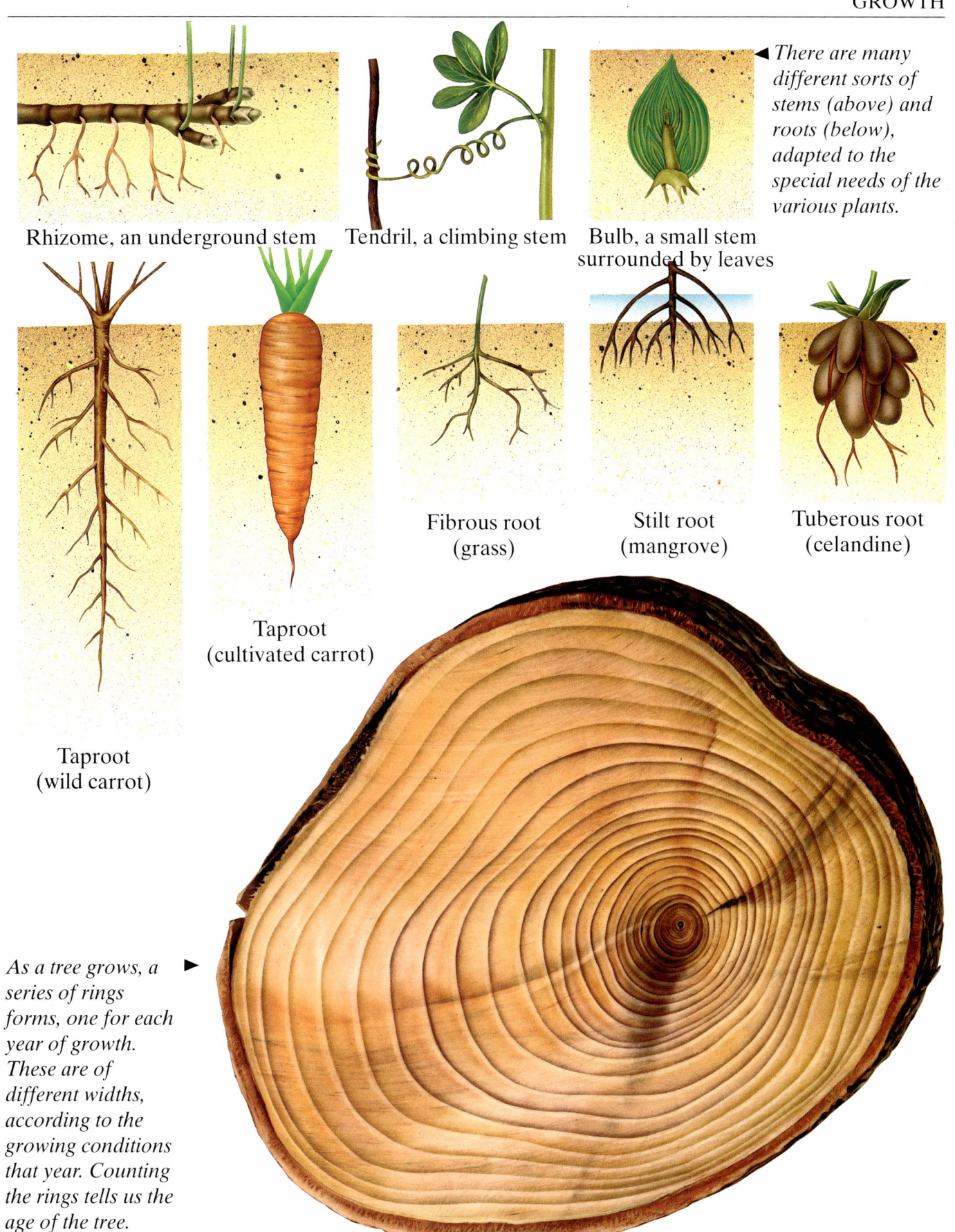

GROWTH

Rhizome, an underground stem

Tendril, a climbing stem

Bulb, a small stem surrounded by leaves

◀ *There are many different sorts of stems (above) and roots (below), adapted to the special needs of the various plants.*

Taproot (cultivated carrot)

Fibrous root (grass)

Stilt root (mangrove)

Tuberous root (celandine)

Taproot (wild carrot)

As a tree grows, a series of rings forms, one for each year of growth. These are of different widths, according to the growing conditions that year. Counting the rings tells us the age of the tree. ▶

5

THE LIFE OF PLANTS

Making or finding food

Green plants are the only living things that are able to make their own food. They take in *water*, *carbon dioxide* and *mineral salts*, and with the aid of the sun's energy, they turn these into the foods they need.

Some plants cannot make their own food. Like animals, they depend on other plants for their existence. These include fungi and some higher plants.

Some of them feed from decaying vegetables and dead animals; these are called *saprophytes*. Parasitic species live off other living things – plants or animals – from which they can obtain the food they need. Rather similar are plants that form a partnership, or *symbiotic* relationship, with others helping them in exchange for food.

Green plants are the first link in the *food chain*. All other living things depend upon them directly or indirectly for food. They provide us with many other useful substances as well.

A grain of starch, like that stored in the tuber of a potato plant. Other plants store oils, fats and so on.

Some plants have a milky juice called latex. It contains stored food and waste products. Rubber is made from latex.

Dodder is a parasite. It starts life rooted in the ground. Then its delicate red stem twines round the host plant and sucks in water and nutrients. With all its needs supplied, its own root withers and dies.

Parasite — Host

Rafflesia is a parasite with no leaves or stems. It gets its food from the roots of other plants. Its flower, up to a metre across, is the biggest of all flowers.

6

MAKING OR FINDING FOOD

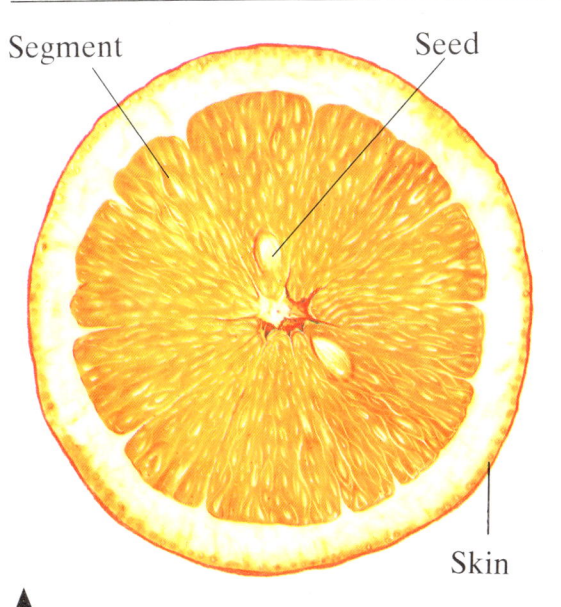

Segment   Seed

Skin

▲
Plants grow and store food in many different ways, and we can often make use of them. The fruit of the orange contains many seeds. Each segment is formed from one carpel. The flesh is delicious to eat and contains much vitamin C.

Green plants use ▶ the sun's energy (*1*) to make their food. Plant-eating animals, or herbivores, (*2*) eat the plants, and they are eaten in turn by meat-eaters, or carnivores (*3*). When they die, their bodies decompose, returning useful substances to the earth (*4*), for the plants' roots to use again.

7

THE LIFE OF PLANTS

Roots and stems

Roots fix the plant in the ground. They also take in water and minerals from the soil, among them nitrogen, phosphorus, iron, calcium and potassium. These substances are vital for the plant as it makes its food.

The journey from the roots to the leaves, where the food is made, can be a very long one. Plants have developed a special kind of *tissue* to carry round water and food. This is known as *vascular tissue*.

Water containing dissolved salts enters the plant through tiny root hairs, near the root tips. From there, it moves from one cell to another until it reaches a tissue called *xylem*. This is made up of long tubes, or vessels, supported by thin fibres. The vessels carry the water up through the stem to the leaves.

At the same time, foods prepared in the leaves during the process known as *photosynthesis* are taken all round the plant through more tube-like cells. These are called *sieve cells*, because the walls between them have little holes through which substances can pass. They are supported by other cells. This tissue is known as *phloem*. The phloem and xylem run close together, with a layer of cells called *cambium* between them.

Each year more vascular tissue is produced in the plant's centre, and more layers of tissue grow around it to protect and support it. The stems of small *herbaceous* plants grow bigger but not harder. Trees and shrubs have *woody* stems. New layers of soft tissue grow in their stems each year and then harden into new rings of wood.

◀ A section cut through the stem of a plant. You can see the long tubes of the xylem which take water up the stem and the sieve tubes of the phloem which carry food from the leaves.

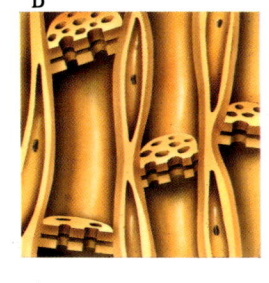

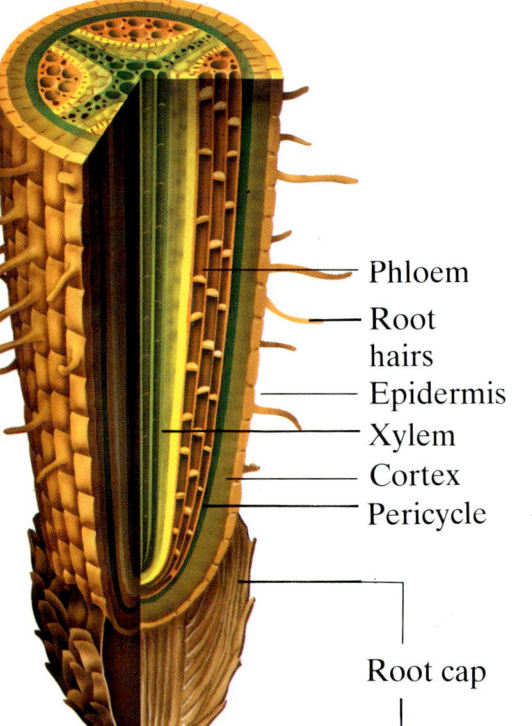

▲ Water and dissolved minerals always travel upwards through the xylem (**A**). Plant food can travel in all directions through the sieve tubes of the phloem (**B**).

- Phloem
- Root hairs
- Epidermis
- Xylem
- Cortex
- Pericycle
- Root cap

◀ A section of a root, showing the xylem and phloem in the core, and the cortex which contains stored food and water.

ROOTS AND STEMS

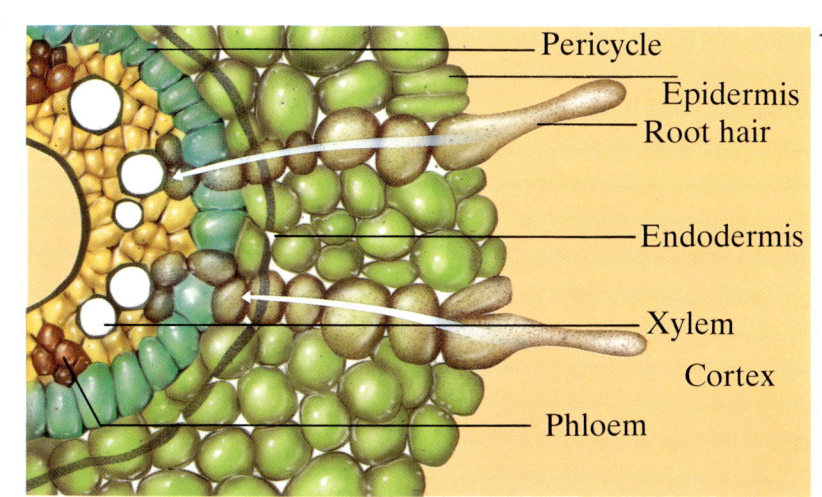

An enlarged section through a young root. Inside the pericycle you can see rows of hollow, dead xylem tubes (yellow and white) and the living cells of the phloem (pink).

Pericycle
Epidermis
Root hair
Endodermis
Xylem
Cortex
Phloem

*A runner bean plant absorbs water containing dissolved mineral salts through its roots (**1**). The cell walls of the roots are very thin and permit water to be absorbed into the xylem in the core of the root. This will carry it up the stem (**2**) to the leaves (**3**), where the process of photosynthesis takes place.*

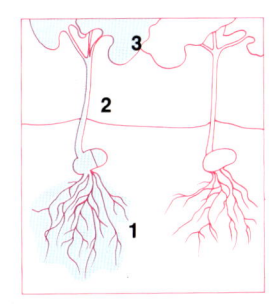

9

THE LIFE OF PLANTS

Leaves

The plant's leaves use the sun's energy to convert carbon dioxide and water into the food that the plant needs to live and develop. This process is known as photosynthesis.

A typical leaf has two parts: the *lamina*, or leaf blade, and the *petiole*, or stalk. Some leaves, however, do not have a petiole, and grow directly from the stem. The leaf absorbs the sun's energy through the lamina, and takes in carbon dioxide from the air.

A leaf has a midrib – an extension of the petiole – and many veins running through it. Through these flow the water absorbed by the root, and the food the plant has made.

Leaves come in many shapes and sizes; some are large and oval, some shaped like needles and so on. Some of them have smooth edges, while others are jagged. Some are thin and flimsy, others are stiff and heavy. They also vary in the way in which they are placed on the stem. Some are opposite each other, some are alternate, some in clusters. Their shapes and arrangements are all adaptations to the conditions in which they usually grow; plants that come from shady places, for example, usually have bigger leaves than ones living in sunny places, so that they can make the most of the weak light.

Plant leaves can be very different from one another. The ones shown here are all simple leaves, with one single blade, but others may be made up of a number of smaller leaflets. These are called compound leaves. ▶

Ginkgo

Red Oak

Evergreen magnolia

Judas tree

Poplar

Japanese maple

Sweet chestnut

Eucalyptus

Holly

Plane

Lime

10

LEAVES

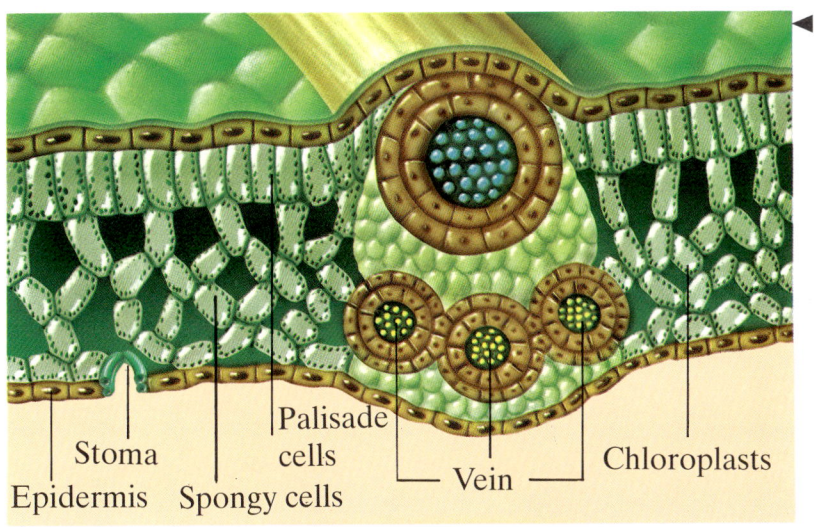

◀ *This section of a leaf shows the layers of different tissues. Just below the leaf surface, or epidermis, is the palisade layer, which has long food-making cells containing many chloroplasts. Below this is a spongy layer which has fewer chloroplasts; the cells are irregular in shape and have spaces between them through which air can circulate. The stoma is one of thousands of tiny breathing holes through which air enters the leaf.*

◀ *Leaves grow from buds on the stem (**1**) of a plant. The leaf blade, or lamina (**2**), is joined to the stem by the stem-like petiole (**3**). The upperside of the leaf (**4**) is usually greener and shinier than the underside (**5**), and it normally faces up to receive the sun's light.*

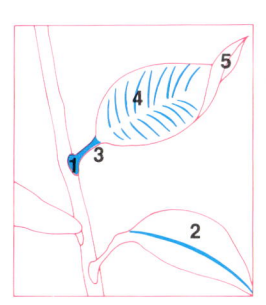

THE LIFE OF PLANTS

Photosynthesis

During photosynthesis plants take in water and carbon dioxide, and use the sun's energy to make *carbohydrates* and *oxygen*. This process takes place in the leaves; it is a very complicated process and we still do not know exactly how it works.

We do, however, know that photosynthesis can take place only in sunlight. Plants trap the sun's energy with *chlorophyll*, a green *pigment* that is found in the chloroplasts in the leaf cells.

Some of the carbohydrates are used to build new cells, and some are stored in the plant as sugars or starch, or turned into other substances, such as fats or pigments. Oxygen produced in photosynthesis is given out by the plant's leaves.

Photosynthesis takes place only during daylight. But another process takes place all the time, even in darkness. This is called *respiration*. In this, some of the carbohydrates are 'burned' by the oxygen to produce energy, and the plant gives out carbon dioxide and water. The plant uses this to make more food and oxygen during photosynthesis.

Plants have other pigments in their leaves, such as *carotene* and *xanthophyll*. These are orange and yellow in colour, but most of the time these colours are masked by the green of the chlorophyll. When the leaves die, however, the chlorophyll is destroyed, and we can see the colours of the other pigments. This is why in autumn the leaves of many plants turn from green to rich shades of red, yellow and brown.

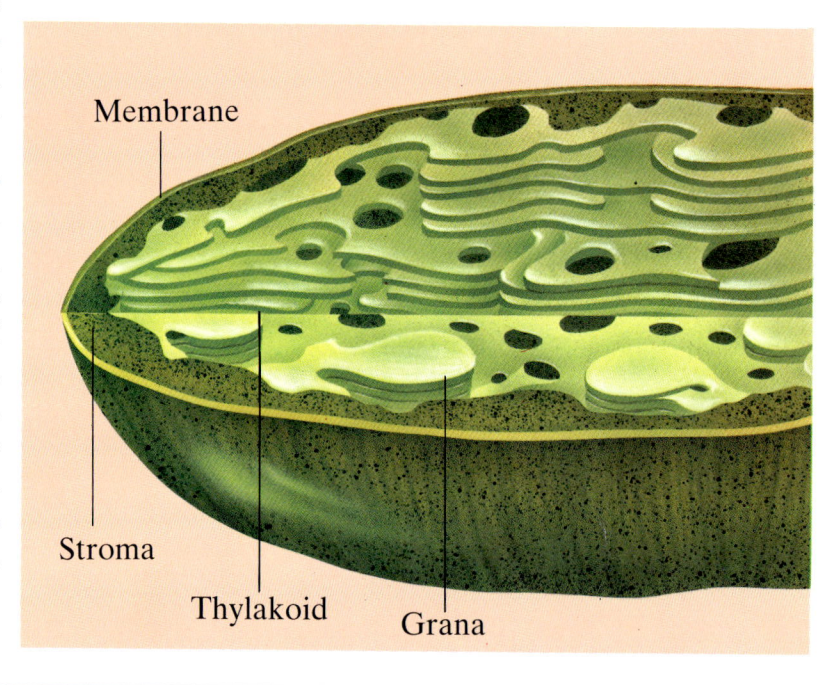

◀ *Potatoes are swollen underground stems, or tubers. They store water and carbohydrate made by the plant during photosynthesis.*

▼ *A chloroplast contains sheets (thylakoids) and stacks (grana) of protein containing the green pigment chlorophyll.*

Membrane

Stroma

Thylakoid

Grana

PHOTOSYNTHESIS

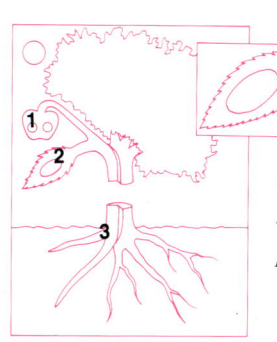

◀ A plant needs carbon dioxide, water and light to make food. A tree's roots (**3**) provide it with water (and minerals) which travel up to the leaves (**2**). There carbohydrates (starch and sugars) are made. The plant uses these products as well as water to form its fruit (**1**). During respiration (inset) the plant uses oxygen given off during photosynthesis to make energy from the food the leaf makes. It gives off carbon dioxide as a waste product.

THE LIFE OF PLANTS

Reproduction

Plants, like animals, must reproduce themselves so that their species will survive. Flowering plants reproduce by forming *seeds*; for this to happen a male cell must join up with a female cell. This is called *sexual reproduction*.

Flowers have male parts and female parts. The male part is formed by the *stamens*. A stamen consists of a delicate *filament*, on one end of which is the *anther* containing the *pollen* grains (sex cells).

The female part of the flower is called the *pistil*, made of one or more carpels. Each carpel is made up of three parts: the *ovary*, within which *ovules* containing sex cells are formed; the *style*; and at its far end, the sticky surfaced *stigma* which will receive the pollen grains. The stamens and the carpels are protected by the *sepals* and the *petals* which make up the *corolla*.

Fertilization, or *pollination*, takes place when pollen grains travel from the stamens to the flower's stigma, and down the style to join the ovule.

Many plants will also grow from *cuttings*. This is one kind of *asexual* reproduction.

Flowers consist of the reproductive parts of the plant surrounded by petals. Before the flower bud opens, it is protected by small leaf-like ◀ *sepals.*

Spike (bear's breech)

Composite (sunflower)

Cyme (stitchwort)

Umbel (wild carrot)

Raceme (shepherd's purse)

14

REPRODUCTION

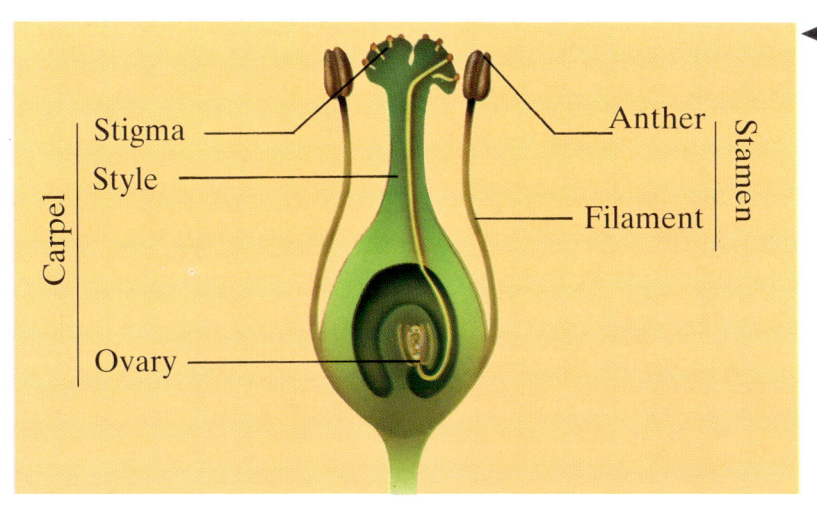

◄ The male and female parts of the flower. The stamen, or male part, is made up of the anther and the filament. The female carpel includes the stigma, style and ovary.

◄ Pollen from the stamen must reach the female part of the flower for fertilization to take place. Some flowers are self pollinating – the pollen can come from the same flowers; others must have pollen from a different flower of the same kind. There are many different ways in which pollen reaches the stigma. In this illustration, a bee has visited a flower and pollen has brushed off on to its hairy body and legs. When it visits another flower, grains of pollen will fall on to the stigma and fertilize it.

THE LIFE OF PLANTS

Pollination and germination

When flowers are fully mature, their anthers open in order to let out pollen grains. Some will be carried to other flowers by insects, others may be blown away by the wind.

When a pollen grain falls on the stigma of a flower, it forms a long tube which goes down through the style until it reaches the ovary. There the pollen fertilizes the ovule and a seed is formed. After it has been fertilized, a flower sheds its petals.

Food from the leaves goes to the ovary and the seed or seeds inside it grow rapidly. The seed contains the *embryo* plant, with a root, a shoot and one or two *seed leaves*, or *cotyledons*. The outside of the seed forms a tough protective coat. The ovaries of plants develop in all sorts of different ways – some become fleshy, some dry out, some grow delicate filaments that can be blown away by the wind.

All these developments are ways of making sure that the plants' seeds are spread round as widely as possible. Fleshy fruits will be eaten by animals, and the seeds dropped miles away; burrs stick to animals and humans, and dandelion seeds and the winged fruits of trees such as sycamores can be blown for great distances. The dry heads of poppies scatter their seeds like pepper pots.

When a seed reaches a nice, moist spot, it *germinates* – sending out a tiny root and shoot which soon grow into a new plant.

Once a flower has been fertilized, its ovary changes and grows. It transforms itself into a fruit. Here you can see some very different types of fruits and seeds.

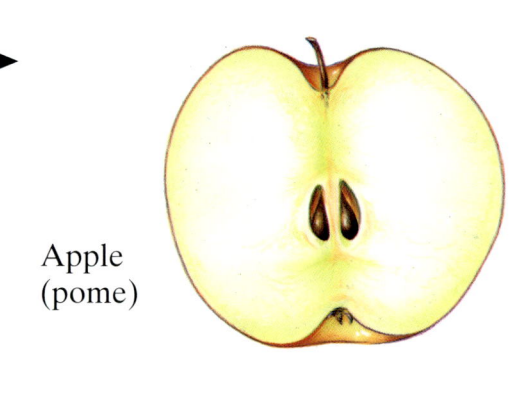

Apple (pome)

Nectarine (drupe)

Lemon (berry)

Wheat grain (indehiscent dry fruit)

Mountain ash (berry)

Pea

(dehiscent dry fruit)

16

POLLINATION AND GERMINATION

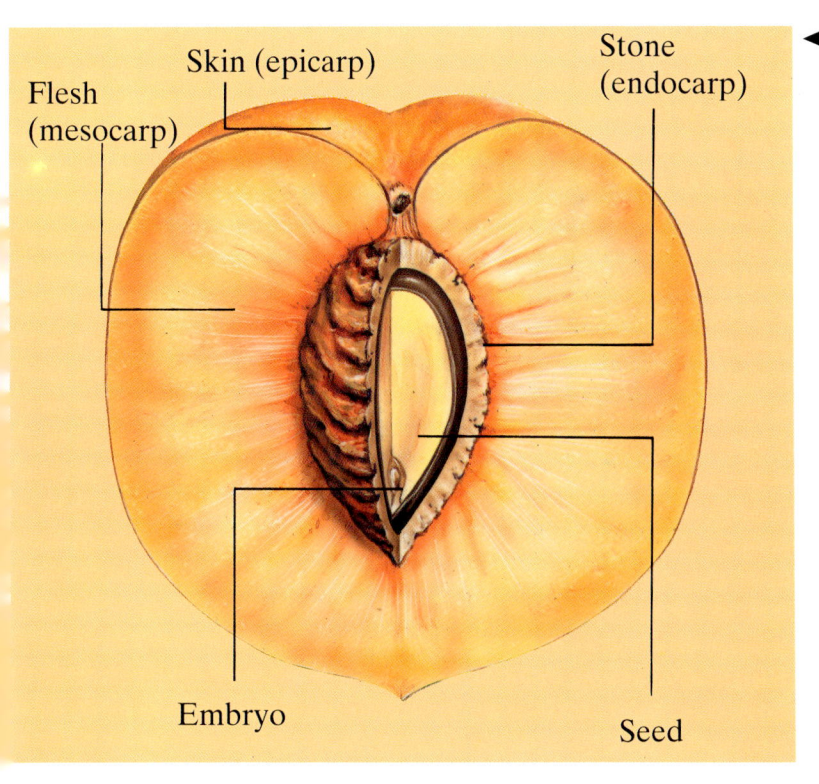

◀ *The inside of a drupe, a fleshy fruit containing a hard 'stone'. The skin is known as the epicarp; the fleshy part of the fruit is called the mesocarp, and the hard shell which covers the seed is called the endocarp.*

*Some plants are capable of self pollination (**1**), but most of them need to receive the pollen of other flowers (**2**); this is called cross pollination.* ▼

THE LIFE OF PLANTS

Transpiration

Some of the water which plants take in through their roots is turned into food, but they also lose a great deal by 'breathing out' water vapour, in a process called *transpiration*. A large tree can lose hundreds of litres of water a day. Some of this water is lost through the stem and flowers, but most of it evaporates from the leaves through little spaces called stomata (singular stoma). The water loss may help to cool the leaves in hot sunshine much as sweating stops us from getting overheated.

Most leaves have flat surfaces through which water vapour easily passes. But plants have adapted in many ways to control water loss when they need to. Many trees, for example, lose their leaves in winter when ground water could be frozen. In others the leaves are reduced to needles with a small surface area and tough surface. Many *cacti* do without leaves altogether. They store water in their stems. *Succulent* plants, which also live in dry places, store water in their thick leaves and stems. They lose little water through their waxy surface.

◄ *A close-up of a stoma flanked by the guard cells that control its opening and closing.*

Plants take in water through their roots, but lose much of it in the form of water vapour through the stomata in their leaves. This passes into the atmosphere. When it rains, some of the water will return to the soil again. This cycle is shown by the arrows in the drawing. ▶

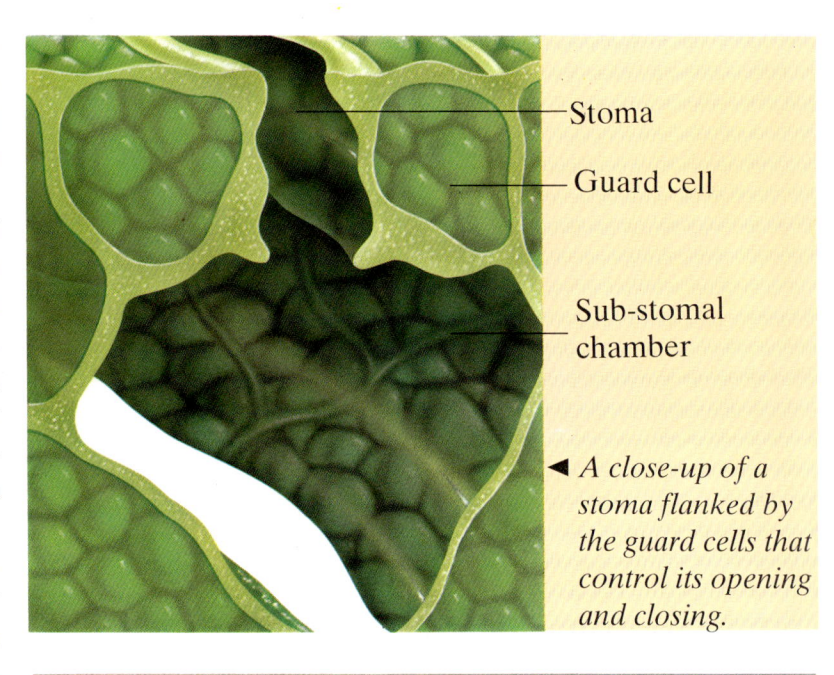

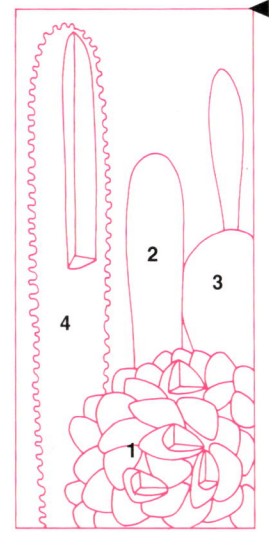

TRANSPIRATION

▶ Many plants living in deserts and other dry environments store large quantities of water. Some store it in their succulent (fleshy) leaves (**1**); others, such as cacti, in their thick stems (**2** & **3**). Many cactus 'leaves' are reduced to little prickles that cannot lose much water. The plant on the left (**4**) is not a cactus, but because it lives in similar conditions, it has developed in a very similar way, with succulent stems and needle-like leaves.

Plants usually lose water in the form of invisible vapour but some may occasionally lose little drops of surplus water through their leaves.
▼

THE LIFE OF PLANTS

Respiration

Plants, like animals, need energy to live; and they get this energy from their food just as we do. The energy is released from the food in the process of respiration, which takes place in the plants cells. Respiration is a kind of burning and it uses oxygen from the air, just as we do and just as a car does to burn its petrol. When food is burned during respiration, it releases carbon dioxide, water and energy.

The main food burned by plants during respiration is glucose, which is a simple kind of sugar. Respiration goes on all the time, but in the daytime, when they are making food by photosynthesis, the plants give out much more oxygen than they use up in respiration.

Most plants need oxygen for respiration; this type of breathing is called *aerobic*. But there are some plants that live where there is no oxygen; they are *anaerobic*. In anaerobic respiration carbohydrates are broken down to form such substances as alcohol or lactic acid. Brewers, for example, use *yeasts* to *ferment* sugars into alcohol. Bacteria can be added to milk to transform its sugars into lactic acid, and this lactic fermentation turns milk into cheese.

Cells are the basic units of all living things – animals as well as plants. A plant cell contains a nucleus and a transparent, jelly-like substance called cytoplasm, surrounded by a cell wall. The nucleus contains the coded information needed to make a new plant and to control the chemical processes and energy production that take place in the cytoplasm. ▶

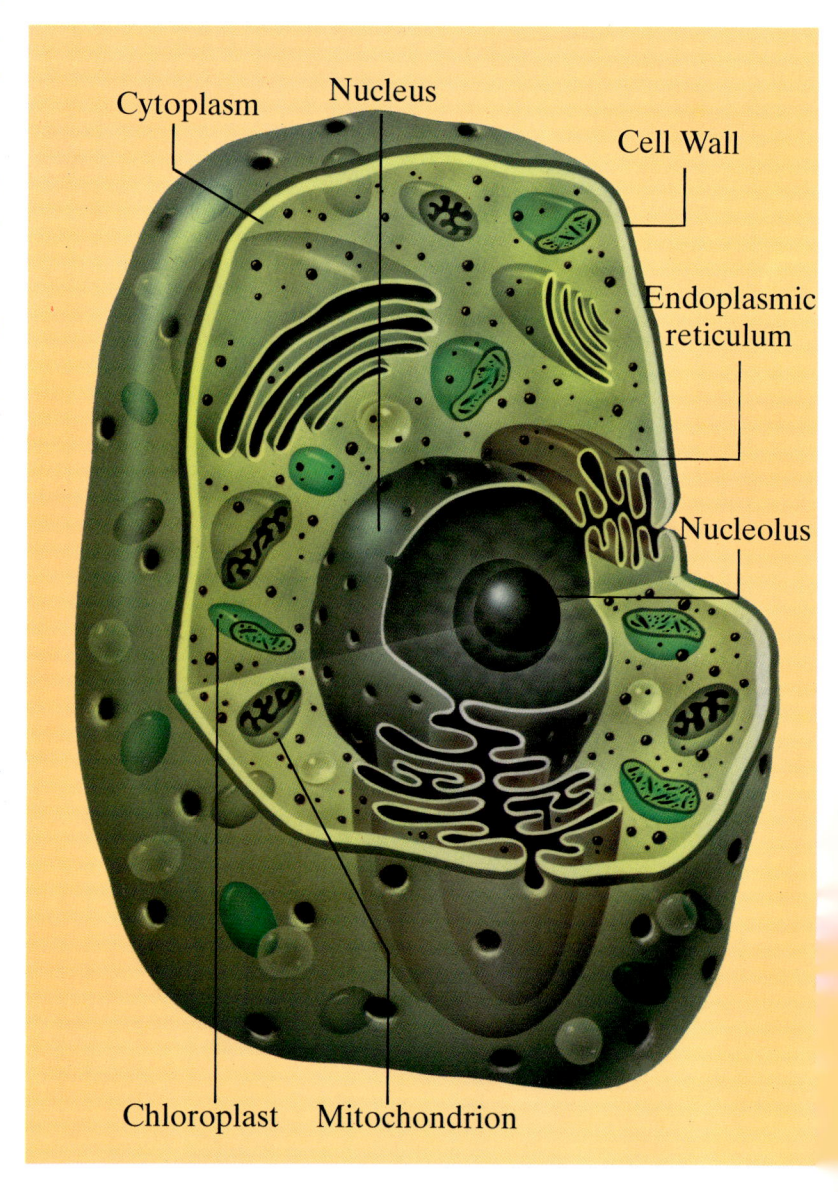

RESPIRATION

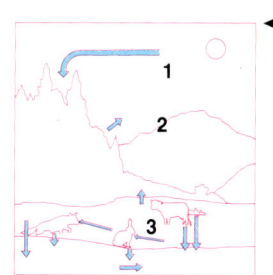

◀ *Plants, animals and soil interact to make up the basic cycles of nature. In the* carbon cycle, *plants absorb carbon dioxide from the atmosphere (**1**) and use it, combined with water which they get from the soil, to make the substances they need for their growth. Animals feed on the plants, and use the carbon in them to build their tissues. Plants and animals give off carbon dioxide when they breathe (**2**), and when they die, the carbon from their bodies goes into the soil (**3**) or back into the air.*

THE LIFE OF PLANTS

Adaptations

Plants live on land and deep under water; in woods, swamps, jungles, mountains and deserts. In order to survive in such different and often difficult conditions, they have developed in some very different and often surprising ways.

In the hot, wet, tropical rainforests, the vegetation is so dense that light hardly filters through to the ground. Here *epiphytic* plants, such as orchids, grow high on the trunks and branches of big trees in order to reach the light. These plants have no soil in which to root; they get their water through their leaves, and through their roots which hang in the humid air. One epiphyte, the bromeliad, collects rain water in a kind of basin formed in the centre of its leaves.

Some plants live completely under water; others have large, floating leaves on the surface. Some have part of their stems and leaves under water, while the rest are above the surface.

Among the strangest are the *insectivorous plants*, which are specially adapted to lure insects into traps and then feed on them.

Epiphytic plants are not rooted in soil on the ground – they grow on the branches and the trunks of other plants. Some ▼ *epiphytes have aerial roots through which they get water and mineral salts. Others, like the bromeliad in the picture, collect and hold water in their leaves.*

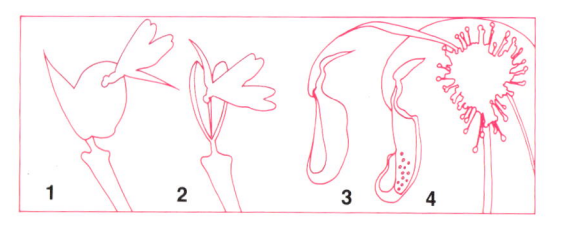

1 2 3 4

22

ADAPTATIONS

Water lilies have large, tough leaves that float on the water's surface and absorb the sun's light. Plants that live under the water usually have long, narrow leaves around which the water can move freely. ▼

◀ Insectivorous plants feed on insects. An insect touches the leaf (**1**); the trap springs shut and the insect is caught inside (**2**). Some species are so designed that the insect falls into a special jug-shaped leaf (**3**). Other species have sticky hairs (**4**) in which the insect gets caught.

THE LIFE OF PLANTS

Plant species

We know of more than 400,000 different species of plant in the world, and there must be many others that we have not yet discovered. Plants come in an almost unbelievable variety of shapes, sizes and colours. Many of them are large and beautiful, but some are tiny and hardly noticeable.

Most plants belong to the group known as the higher plants; they have roots, stems, leaves and produce seeds. They are divided into two groups: *gymnosperms* and *angiosperms*.

Gymnosperms have no true flowers, and their seeds are not enclosed in a fruit. The best known are the *conifers* – firs, pines and so on.

Angiosperms have flowers, and their seeds are enclosed inside a fruit. There are two groups of angiosperms: the *dicotyledons* and the *monocotyledons*. These are named after the number of leaves in the seed: the dicotyledons have two seed leaves, the monocotyledons have one.

Monocotyledon (wheat)

Dicotyledon (bean)

◀ *The seed of an angiosperm is formed inside the ovary, which matures and transforms itself into a fruit. The embryo which develops can have one seed leaf (cotyledon) or two; the plants are known as monocotyledons or dicotyledons.*

◀ *Conifers are the most numerous of the gymnosperms. Most species are evergreen and have needle-shaped leaves. They carry their seeds in woody cones.*

Pine cone

Female cone

Male cone

Sections through the female cone (left) and male cone (right) of a conifer. Ovules form on the scales of the female cone and pollen on the scales of the male cone.

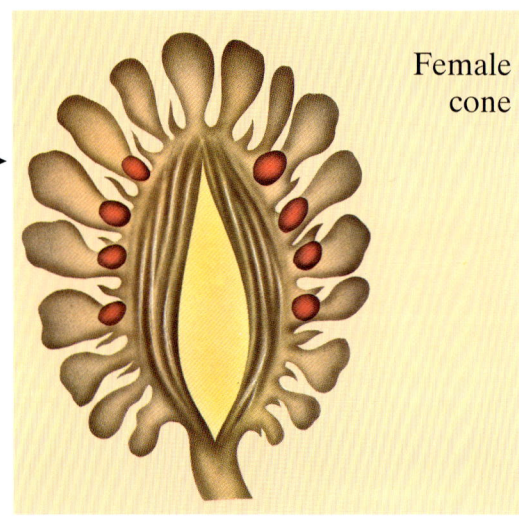

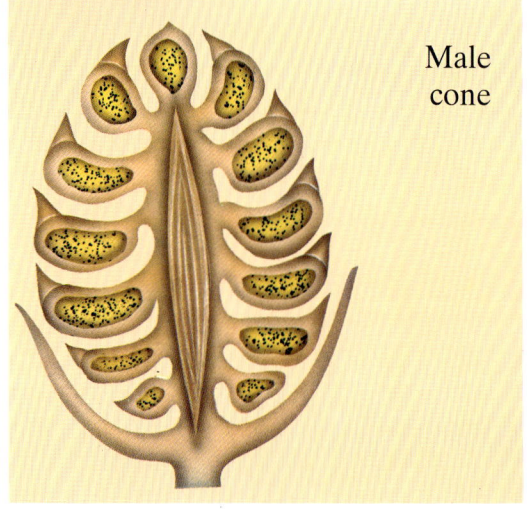

PLANT SPECIES

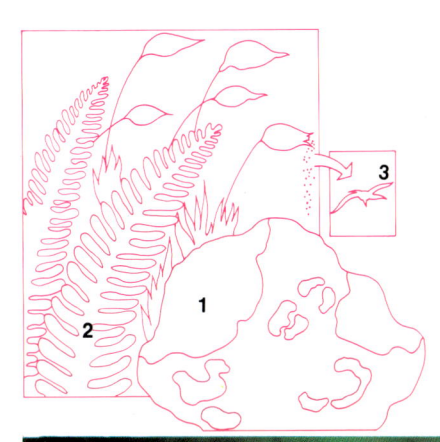

▼ Lichens (**1**) are combinations of algae and fungi living together in partnership (symbiosis). They grow on the ground, on tree trunks, on rocks and so on. They have neither flowers nor seeds, and they reproduce by spores, as do mosses and ferns. The spores are found on the underside of the leaves, or fronds, (**2**) of the ferns and in spore capsules on the mosses (**3**). When the moss spores are mature, they fall to the ground, where they germinate and each develops into a branching thread called a protonema. Buds grow on this and develop into a new clump of moss.

THE LIFE OF PLANTS

Plant products

Look around you and see how many everyday things come from plants. Cotton and linen fibres are used in your clothes, and hemp, jute and coconut fibres in rope, sacking and matting. Trees provide wood for furniture, for the frames and windows of houses, and for fuel. The paper this book is printed on is made from wood pulp.

Many familiar medicines such as penicillin come from plants. Perfumes are made from their flowers and leaves, and flowers, leaves, stems and bark are all used to dye cloth. Above all, of course, plants provide most of the food we eat.

But not all plant products are good for us. Some are very poisonous. Nightshade berries, laburnum seeds and some fungi can kill you. And deadly drugs such as heroin and cocaine come from plants.

People have been cultivating plants for thousands of years. They have carefully chosen the strongest and healthiest plants, and those that gave the highest yields. They have learned how to breed new varieties, which will have the best qualities of their parents, or which will grow in poor conditions. All the time, new varieties are being created to meet our needs.

Aloe

Jojoba

◄ Products, such as oils, perfumes and so on, are extracted from certain plants.

► Through carefully selecting and breeding from the best plants, people have developed new large, disease-resistant varieties. See the difference between the wild carrot (**1**) and the cultivated one (**2**), between the cultivated maize (**3**) and the uncultivated one (**4**), and cultivated (**5**) and wild wheat (**6**).

26

PLANT PRODUCTS

Jute Hemp Flax

Fibres from jute, hemp, flax and cotton are used in the manufacture of cloth, ropes, bags and so on. ◄

Cotton

Some plants, such ► *as the olive (top) and the sunflower (right), have useful oils in their fruits (olives) or seeds (sunflowers).*

THE LIFE OF PLANTS

Finding out

There are all sorts of experiments you can carry out with plants, and parts of plants, that will help you to understand how they grow and function. You will not need any unusual equipment for most of them, just a few seeds, leaves and so on, and a few jars and plastic bags that you will find around the house.

Germination
Even the tiniest of seeds carries within its protective covering the beginnings of a whole new plant, which only needs the right conditions to grow. The first essentials for growth are moisture and oxygen (this is why many seeds are packed in airtight foil envelopes).

Take a jar, and place some damp cotton wool in the bottom. Rest a seed on it – not a very tiny seed that would be hard to see, but something the size of a pea. The seed will absorb water, and the cells of the embryo within it will start to divide until the outer covering of the seed splits open.

The first thing to appear will be a little white root. This is the *radicle*. Then a little shoot called the *plumule* appears and starts to grow upwards. This will turn into the stem, and leaves will later grow from it.

Placing seeds in a glass jar, on damp cotton wool, gives them the conditions they need to start growing (germination). The glass allows you to watch what is happening!
▼

How a bean seed ▶ *grows. First the radicle grows down; then the plumule grows up, while more roots grow out from the radicle. Whichever way up you place the seed, the radicle always grows down, and the plumule up.*

FINDING OUT

How leaves lose water

As we have seen, plants lose a great deal of water vapour through their leaves, in the process known as transpiration. Most of it passes out through tiny holes in the leaves, called stomata.

Take a young plant in a pot, and water the soil well. Place a clear, airtight plastic bag over the plant. Then fasten it tightly round the stem with an elastic band or a piece of string. Very soon, the plastic will mist over with moisture breathed out by the plant's leaves, until drops of water run down inside it.

Absorbing minerals

Plants take up water containing mineral salts from the soil through their roots; it travels up the stem to the leaves where it is used to make the plant's food. A stick of celery placed in water coloured with red ink will help you to see how quickly water moves up the plant's vascular tissue. You can dye a white carnation pink or blue using the same technique.

◀ *Where does the moisture in the air- and watertight plastic bag come from? It is water vapour which has been breathed out by the leaves of the young geranium plant. The water was taken in by its roots from the damp soil, and travelled up through the stem, along the stalks and into the leaves.*

◀ *Fill a glass with water coloured red with ink, and then stand a stalk of celery in it. You will see that, before long, the red colour of the ink begins to show up in the stem and finally in the leaves.*

If you cut a slice ▶ *through the celery stem, you will be able to see the red-stained vascular tissue through which the water has travelled.*

Index and glossary

Adaptation 22,23
Aerobic respiration 20
A chemical reaction, using oxygen, which takes place in plants and releases carbon dioxide, water and energy.
Anaerobic respiration 20
A chemical reaction which takes place in certain plants to release energy when no oxygen is available.
Angiosperms 24
A group of plants with roots, stems, leaves and flowers, the seeds of which are enclosed in an ovary.
Anther 14,15,16
The part of the stamen which contains the pollen grains.
Asexual reproduction 14
Reproduction which does not depend on the joining of male and female sex cells; some simple plants reproduce by asexual structures called spores, and gardeners reproduce plants asexually by budding or by taking cuttings.
Bacteria 20
Breeding 26
Bromeliad 22
Bulb 5
Cactus/cacti 18,19
Succulent plants with thick, fleshy stems and clusters of spines growing from little 'cushions'.
Calcium 8
Cambium 8
The layer of tissue in a root or stem, which produces the new cells responsible for the increase in thickness.
Carbohydrates 12,13
Compounds of carbon, hydrogen and oxygen which are plentiful in plants and animals; as foods they produce heat and energy and they make up the framework of some structures. Examples include sugar and starch.
Carbon cycle 21
Carbon dioxide is taken from the air by plants and used to make food. Animals eat the plants and breathe out carbon dioxide into the air while alive and return carbon to the soil when they die and decompose.
Carbon dioxide 6,10,12,13,20,21
A gas taken into a plant from the air, and combined with water during photosynthesis to produce sugars.
Carotene 12
A yellow pigment found in plants.
Carpel 7,14
The female reproductive organ of a plant: it consists of a flattened stigma at the top, and a narrow tube called the style leading down to a round base called the ovary in which egg cells form.
Chlorophyll 12
The green pigment found in plants which absorbs energy from sunlight.
Chloroplast 11
Minute component of a plant cell, containing chlorophyll. Photosynthesis takes place in the chloroplasts.
Conifer 24
Tree belonging to the group called gymnosperms, including pines, firs and cypresses. They have needle-shaped leaves, and almost all of them are evergreen. They bear their seeds in cones, which gives them their name.
Corolla 14
The petals of a flower, which may be separate as in a buttercup or joined together as in a columbine.
Cortex 8
Cotyledon 16
A special form of leaf, also known as a seed leaf, often containing food reserves, which is part of the embryo in the seed.
Cutting 14
Shoot of a growing plant which, when planted and carefully looked after, will grow roots and turn into a plant identical to its parent.
Dicotyledons 24
Plants whose seeds contain two cotyledons, or seed leaves.
Dodder 6
Embryo 16
The rudimentary plant contained in a seed.
Epidermis 11
The outer layer of living cells in plant structures.
Epiphyte 22
A plant growing perched on a tree and absorbing moisture from the air instead of from the soil.
Fermentation 20
A chemical change caused by yeasts in which alcohol and carbon dioxide are produced from sugars.
Fertilization 14,16
The joining of male and female sex cells to form the first cell of a new plant.
Fibres 26,27
Fibrous root 5
Filament 14,15
The long, narrow stalk of the stamen that supports the anther.
Flower 4,10,14,15
The part of a plant containing its reproductive organs, including stamens, carpels, calyx and corolla.
Food 6,7,16
Food chain 6
The sequence in which one animal feeds on plants and is then eaten by another which is in turn eaten by another. Every food chain starts with a plant.
Frond 25
Fruit 16,17
Fungus/fungi 6
Plants, lacking chlorophyll, that live as parasites or saprophytes, taking food from living or dead plants or animals.
Germinate See Germination

INDEX AND GLOSSARY

Germination 16,17,28
The beginning of growth from a seed.
Growth 4,5
Gymnosperms 24
Plants whose seeds are not enclosed in an ovary.
Herbaceous 8
Describes non-woody plants that die down at the end of the growing season.
Higher plants 4,24
Plants that have roots, stems, leaves and seeds.
Insectivorous 22,23
Describes insect-eating plants.
Iron 8
Lamina 10
The leaf blade.
Latex 6
Leaves 4,10,11,13,18,19,22-25
The parts of a plant in which the food-making process called photosynthesis takes place.
Lichens 25
Organisms formed by the combination of a fungus and a green alga.
Minerals 8,23
Mineral salts 6,9,22,29
Mineral compounds dissolved in water, taken in by the roots of a plant.
Monocotyledons 24
Plants whose seeds have only one cotyledon, or seed leaf.
Moss 25
Nitrogen 8
Oils 26,27
Orchids 22
Ovary 14,15,16
The part of the flower carpel containing the ovules.
Ovules 14,16,24
Structures in the ovary that contain the female cells and develop into seeds when they are fertilized.
Oxygen 12,13,20
A gas made by the plant during photosynthesis and breathed out through the stomata.

Parasite 6
An organism which does not make its own food but gets it from a living host.
Pericycle 9
Petals 14,16
Divisions of the corolla of a flower.
Petiole 10
The stalk joining the leaf to the stem.
Phloem 8
Tube-like tissue that carries foods made in the leaves throughout the plant.
Phosphorus 8
Photosynthesis 8,9,10,12,13
The process in which plants convert carbon dioxide, water and dissolved minerals into food, using the sun's energy.
Pigment 12
A colouring matter or substance.
Pistil 14
The female part of a flower, consisting of one or more carpels.
Plant cell 20
Plant products 26
Plant species 24,25
Plumule 28
The first shoot that develops from the seed.
Pollen 14,15,16
Grains produced in the plant's anther which develop male sex cells.
Pollination 15,16,17
The transfer of pollen from the stamen of a flower to the stigma of the same or another flower.
Potassium 8
Potatoes 12
Protein 12
Radicle 28
The first root developed from the seed.
Rafflesia 6
Reproduction 14,15
Respiration 12,13,20,21
The process that takes place inside the plant, in which oxygen and glucose combine to produce energy, releasing carbon dioxide and water.
Rhizome 5
Roots 4,5,8,9,13,22
The structures that anchor a plant in the ground and take in water and dissolved nutrients.
Runner bean 9
Saprophyte 6
Plant that takes its food from decomposing animal or vegetable material.
Seed 14,15,16,17,24,28
The ripe ovule of a plant.
Seed leaves See Cotyledo
Sepals 14
Outermost parts of a flower that protect the petals when the flower is in bud.
Sexual reproduction 14
The uniting of male sex cells from pollen with female sex cells in the ovary.
Sieve cells 8
Cells forming tubes which carry nutrients around the plant, divided from one another by walls containing little holes.
Spores 25
Stamen 14,15
The male reproductive organ of a plant, consisting of an anther on the end of a narrow filament.
Stem 4,8,9,18,19,29
The part of the plant which supports its leaves and flowers.
Stigma 14,15
The flattened structure at the top of the pistil, on which pollen grains are deposited.
Stilt root 5
Stoma/stomata 11,18,29
Small holes in the surface of a plant's leaves, through which pass carbon dioxide, oxygen and water vapour.
Style 14,15
The narrow tube of the carpel, joining the stigma and the ovary.
Succulent 18
Describes plants with thick, fleshy leaves that retain moisture.

THE LIFE OF PLANTS

Symbiosis 6,25
A partnership, or symbiotic relationship, of living organisms, in which both benefit.
Symbiotic See Symbiosis
Taproot 5
Tendril 5
Tissue 8
Collection of specialized cells or fibres forming structures in a plant or animal.
Transpiration 18,19,29
The process in which plants lose water vapour.
Tree rings 5
Tuberous root 5
Vascular tissue 8,29
The tube-like structures called xylem and phloem that carry water, nutrients etc round the plant.
Water 6,8,9,10,12,13,18-23, 29
A compound of hydrogen and oxygen that plants and all living things need to live.
Water lilies 23
Woody stems 8
The rigid stems of trees and shrubs; unlike the non-woody herbaceous plants, they contain large amounts of xylem.
Xanthophyll 12
A yellow pigment in leaves.
Xylem 8,9
Tissue made up of long tubes through which water and dissolved substances travel up the plant from the roots to the leaves.
Yeasts 20
Tiny single-celled fungi which are important in fermentation.